Contents

What is a force?

Forces are the pushes and pulls that make things move, stop moving, change direction, or stay still. Whatever's happening, forces are making it happen.

Even when you're sitting still like this, lots of forces are at work:

- Gravity is pulling you down
- Friction makes you able to hold your book
- You're being squeezed by air pressure from the air all around you
- Even inside your brain, forces make signals zoom around between your brain cells, so you can understand what you're looking at.

To see a force in action, find something small and unbreakable, like an eraser.

Pick it up...

You create a pulling force to make the object move upwards, using your hand.

Now drop it!

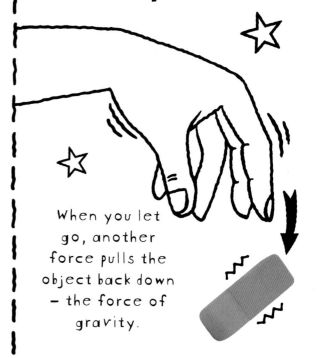

When you let go, another force pulls the object back down – the force of gravity.

Understanding forces

Scientists have been studying forces for centuries, to find out how they work.

Agnes Pockels (1862-1935) did experiments on the surface tension of water.

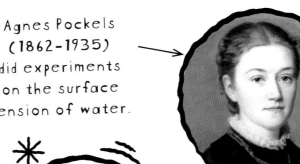

I ALSO DISCOVERED JUPITER'S MOONS!

Isaac Newton (1642-1727), the most famous forces boffin of all time, came up with many rules and formulas that show how forces work.

Galileo Galilei (1564-1642) worked on how things fall and speed up.

I HELPED PUT HUMANS ON THE MOON!

Katherine Johnson (1918-) calculated flight paths and orbits for spacecraft.

Inventions and discoveries

Understanding forces allows us to invent, build and control all kinds of brilliantly useful inventions, too...

Rockets

Bicycles   Brakes

Seesaws

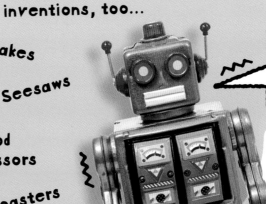

AND ROBOTS! THE LIST IS ENDLESS!

Food processors

Helicopters

Bridges   Rollercoasters

Why doesn't the Moon fall down?

Moon

The Moon is a ginormous ball made of about 73,500 trillion kg of rock. So have you ever wondered…

What's holding it up??

The Moon is the Earth's constant companion, always sailing peacefully around the sky.

But HOW?

Well…

The Earth has a powerful pulling force, the force of gravity.

Gravity pulls you and other objects down to the ground.

WOOF!
WOOF!
WOOF!

Mass

All objects have mass – meaning the matter, or stuff, they are made of. The more mass an object has, the more gravity it has.

The Earth is a huge planet with lots of mass. Its powerful gravity reaches far out into space.

The Moon is smaller than the Earth, but it is pretty big and has its own gravity too.

LET ME GO!

As the Moon moves, it tries to pull away in a straight line.

The Earth and Moon both pull on each other. So, you might think they would just pull and pull until they crashed together...right?

However...

There's another force involved too. The Moon is also moving at high speed.

As the Moon zooms forward, it tries to pull away from the Earth and fly off in a straight line. But gravity pulls it towards the Earth at the same time. The two forces are in balance, so the Moon just keeps circling, or orbiting, the Earth.

Orbits are everywhere!

Other planets also have moons orbiting them. The planets themselves orbit around the Sun. And we send rockets and satellites into orbit too. For example, the International Space Station (ISS) is in orbit 400 km from Earth. Scientists live aboard it for months at a time.

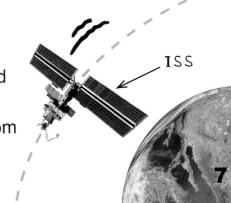

ISS

Why does rubbing your hands together warm them up?

Brrrrr...

It's freezing and you've forgotten your gloves! Rub your hands together, and they should start to feel a bit warmer.

This handy heating method exists thanks to one of the most important forces of all: **friction**.

The rubbing force

Friction is a force that slows down or stops things when they rub, scrape or slide together.

For example...

- Rubber gloves help you grip a tight jar lid
- Brakes rub against the wheels to slow down a bike
- Trainers grip the ground.

Basically, if it wasn't for friction, we'd all be slipping and sliding around all over the place!

Rough stuff

Friction happens because surfaces are never completely smooth. Even if they look and feel smooth, through a microscope you'd see they have a rough surface.

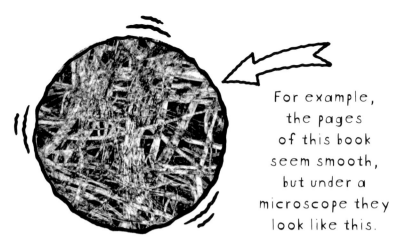

For example, the pages of this book seem smooth, but under a microscope they look like this.

But where does the heat come from?

When surfaces rub together, they get pushed and squeezed. This makes the molecules in the materials start moving around faster. When the molecules in a material move faster, the material becomes hotter – and that's what happens to your hands.

Burning up!

Friction can sometimes make things a LOT hotter than warm hands on a winter's day. Like…

… if you slide down a rope too fast, it makes your hands so hot you get a 'friction burn' …

…and rubbing sticks together can (eventually) start a fire!

Hot money!

This simple experiment will amaze you!

Put two matching coins on a pad of paper. Put one index finger on one coin, and one on the other.

Hold one coin still, and rub the other one hard to and fro on the paper for ten seconds.

Compare the coins. Is one warmer?

Why don't pond skaters fall in?

Look closely at a pond on a summer's day, and you'll see pond skaters zipping around on the surface.

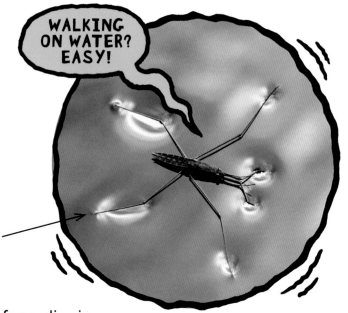

WALKING ON WATER? EASY!

They're not floating like boats (see pages 14-15). They're actually STANDING on the water!

You can even see the water surface dipping where the pond skater's feet press on it. It's as if the water has a thin, stretchy skin.

Where's the skin?
Water doesn't actually have a skin. If it did, you'd find it in your glass when you had a drink.

Eeeww!

Instead, water just **acts** as if it has a skin, because of surface tension.

10

Look inside...

Surface tension happens because of cohesive forces. Water, like everything else, is made of tiny molecules. Cohesive forces pull the molecules towards each other.

At the surface, the forces only pull each molecule from the sides and below.

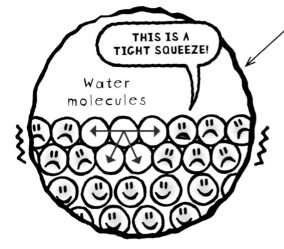

THIS IS A TIGHT SQUEEZE!

Water molecules

In the middle of the water, the forces pull each molecule in all directions.

This pulls the molecules at the surface inwards and closer together, and they act like a skin. Surface tension is quite weak – you can still break through it easily. But it will support a little weight.

Try it yourself...

To test surface tension, fill a bowl with water, wait until it's still, then gently lower a small paper clip onto the surface.

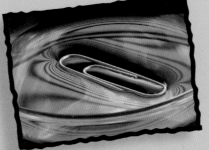

Metal objects like these paper clips don't float, but the surface tension can hold them up.

Drip... drop...

Surface tension is also the reason water forms round drops. A small amount of water pulls itself into a ball. Or, if it's on a flat surface, it forms a dome.

How does a parachute save your life?

Jumping out of a plane without a parachute would be seriously bad news. But if you had a parachute, you'd be fine – even if you fell thousands of metres!

GOING DOWN!

Tiny air particles

Going down!
If you jump out of a plane, the Earth's gravity pulls you down, so you fall quickly towards the ground.

BUMP!

BUMP!

BUMP!

But, as you fall through the air, you hit millions of tiny, invisible air particles. They push against you and slow you down a bit (but not much).

This is called air resistance or drag. It's a type of friction (see pages 8–9).

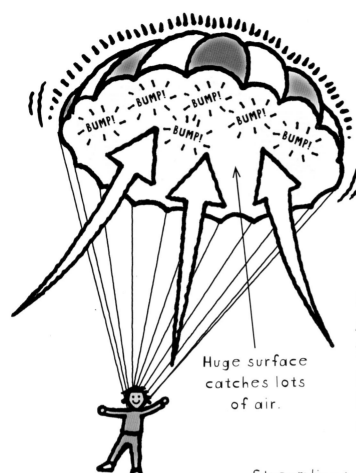

Huge surface catches lots of air.

Slow me down!

The bigger your surface area, the more particles you'll hit, and the slower you'll go. A parachute has a really big surface area, and lots of air resistance – making the fall slow enough to be safe.

Speed me up!

Air resistance slows down anything that moves through air – like planes, cars and bikes. So vehicles have pointed, smooth, 'streamlined' shapes, to reduce air resistance.

Streamlined shapes let air flow past them easily.

Water resistance

The same thing happens in water, except the resistance is even stronger, as water is thicker. Many sea creatures, like penguins, have a streamlined shape to help them go faster.

Streamlined penguin

We make submarines this shape too.

How can a metal boat float?

Container ship

Drop a steel nail into water and it will sink. Yet a massive steel ocean-going container ship floats. What's that about?!

Steel nail

To see why this happens, you have to start with why things float. It's all to do with how dense materials are – that is, how heavy they are for their size.

Why steel sinks

To float, an object has to be less dense than water.

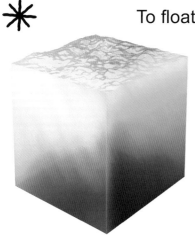

A litre of water like this, measuring 10cm x 10 cm x 10 cm, weighs 1 kg.

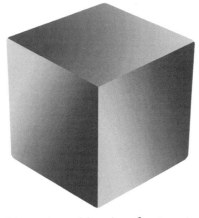

Here's a block of steel the exact same size – but it weighs 7.9 kg! It's much denser than the water...

...so it sinks!

Why wood floats

Now let's try it with a block of wood the same size.

...so it floats!

The wood block weighs about 0.4 kg – it's less dense than water...

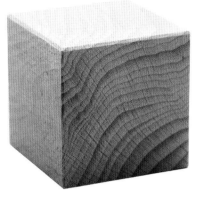

Upthrust

When you put an object in water, the water pushes back up against it, with a force called upthrust. But the upthrust can only hold up objects that are less dense than water. It can't support denser objects, so they sink.

Brilliant boats

HOWEVER, boats can float, even steel boats. That's because of their shape.

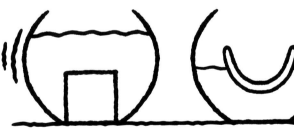

A solid lump of steel sinks, because it's denser than water.

But a boat is shaped like a bowl, with air in the middle.

The density of the whole shape isn't just steel. It also includes the air inside. All the air makes the overall density much lower –

so the boat floats!

Floating metals

The metals lithium, sodium and potassium are actually less dense than water, and can float. However, they don't make great boats as they explode when they touch water!

BANG!

How can a plane fly upside down?

You might have heard that planes fly because of the shape of their wings. But if that's how planes fly, then flying upside down should surely make them fall to the ground!

But many planes CAN fly upside down... like this one!

How?

Many aircraft wings do have a special shape, called an aerofoil. It's shaped like this:

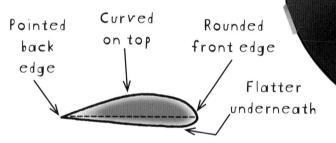

Pointed back edge

Curved on top

Rounded front edge

Flatter underneath

This shape makes air zoom over the top of the wing much faster than the bottom. Faster-moving air presses less hard, so there's less air pressure on the top of the wing than on the bottom, and that gives the wing lift.

Lift is a force that pushes upwards, against gravity.

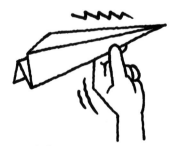

But...

There's something else that's actually much more important for making a plane fly, and that's the angle of the wings.

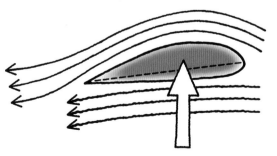

After all, a paper aeroplane just has flat wings. But it will fly for a while if you throw it at the right angle.

Angle of attack

As a plane flies along, its wings are angled slightly upwards at the front.

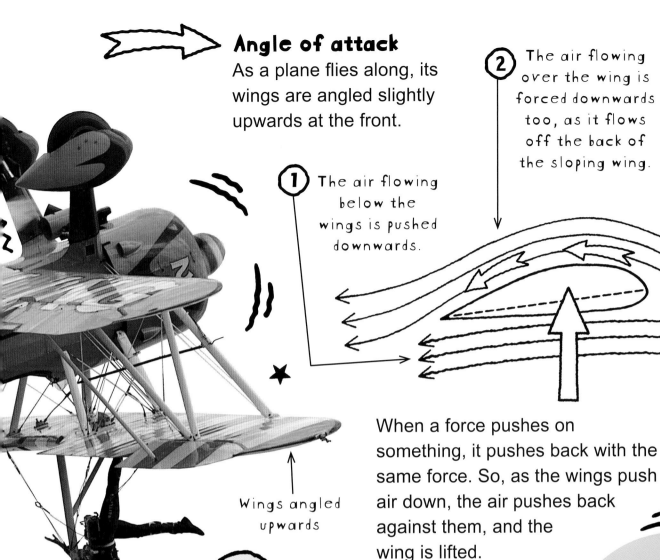

① The air flowing below the wings is pushed downwards.

② The air flowing over the wing is forced downwards too, as it flows off the back of the sloping wing.

Wings angled upwards

MIND MY HEAD!

When a force pushes on something, it pushes back with the same force. So, as the wings push air down, the air pushes back against them, and the wing is lifted.

Invert!

Stunt pilots call upside-down flight 'inverted'. To do it, they have to fly with the nose of the plane pointing up slightly, so that the wings are still angled upwards.

Equal and opposite

It was the brilliant scientist Isaac Newton who explained how, when a force acts on something, it pushes back with an equal force in the opposite direction.

IT'S CALLED MY (NEWTON'S) THIRD LAW OF MOTION!

Why can't people grow as big as dinosaurs?

Brachiosaurus

Imagine being 12 metres tall – as tall as a four-storey building! Giants in myths and movies can be this big, and so were some dinosaurs.

So why aren't there any giant humans?

Real-life giants

The tallest man on record was Robert Wadlow, who grew to 2.72 m.

Average human height is around 1.65 m, so Wadlow did look giant – but he was still less than twice average height for a human. Real giants, the height of a brachiosaurus, don't exist – for a very good reason...
...**FORCES!**

Life in 3D

If you were 12 m tall like a brachiosaurus, you'd be about seven times taller than average. But humans are 3D objects. If you were seven times taller, you wouldn't just be seven times heavier. You'd be much, **MUCH** heavier.

Here's how it works.

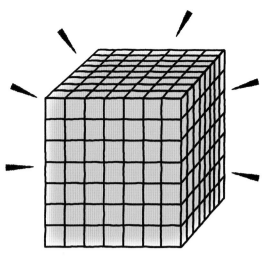

(1) Think of a cube…

(2) Now imagine a cube twice as tall. It wouldn't be twice as heavy – it would be **8** times heavier.

(3) And a cube seven times taller would be **343** times heavier!

Human bones are strong, but not **THAT** strong. If you were 12 m tall, the bones in your legs would have to carry so much weight that they would crumble. Even though your bones would be bigger too, they wouldn't be hundreds of times stronger.

So how did brachiosaurus do it?

Hollow bones in its back, neck and tail made its skeleton lighter.

Its body shape helped to carry its huge weight.

Four legs spread its weight.

Tall towers

We have to think about this when we build huge towers and skyscrapers. Engineers calculate the forces on all the parts of the tower, and make sure the materials used are strong enough to withstand them. Otherwise...

Crash!

Why is falling off a cliff so deadly?

Jumping off a chair or a small wall is (usually!) pretty safe, but falling off a cliff or high building definitely isn't. The reason is all to do with gravity.

Falling down... speeding up

When an object falls, the Earth's gravity pulls it down to the ground. But as objects fall, they also accelerate, or get faster and faster. This is called the 'acceleration of gravity', or **g**.

Here's how **g** works. Imagine dropping a small rock off a cliff.

 (Just imagine it, though — DON'T ever do it, as it could land on someone!)

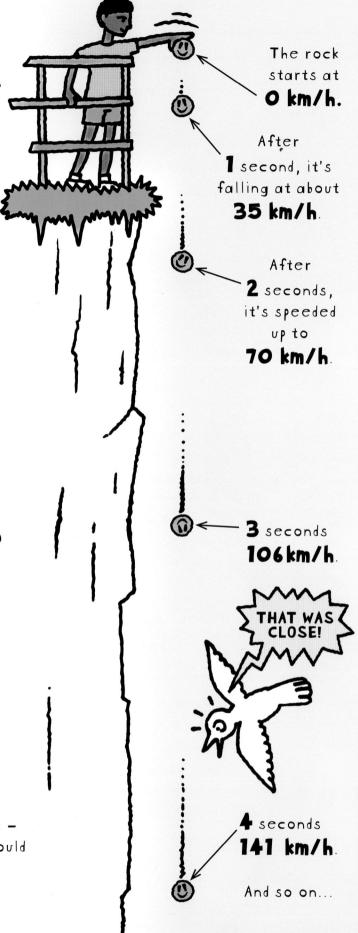

The rock starts at **0 km/h.**

After **1** second, it's falling at about **35 km/h**.

After **2** seconds, it's speeded up to **70 km/h**.

3 seconds **106 km/h**.

THAT WAS CLOSE!

4 seconds **141 km/h**.

And so on...

If a rock fell off a 100-m-high cliff, it would take about 4.5 seconds to get to the bottom. By the time it landed, it would be travelling at 158 km/h. That's **FAST** – as fast as a high-speed train.

THAT WAS QUICK!

Top speed!

In real life, falling objects don't keep speeding up forever. As an object falls faster, it hits the air harder, and there's more air resistance. Eventually, the object reaches its maximum possible speed, or 'terminal velocity'.

For a falling human, such as a skydiver, terminal velocity is about 200 km/h.

Sky spider

DON'T WORRY, I'LL BE FINE!

Smaller, lighter animals have more surface area for their weight, so there's more air resistance and they don't reach a very high speed.

So, for example, a spider could fall off a skyscraper, and survive without injury.

How can a magnet pull something it's not... *touching?*

Magnets pull towards each other, or push each other away – depending on which way round you hold them.

It's like magic! Or IS it.....?

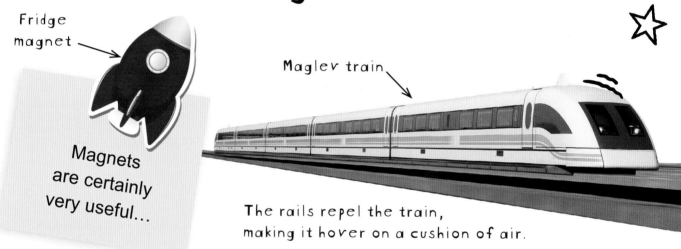

Fridge magnet

Magnets are certainly very useful...

Maglev train

The rails repel the train, making it hover on a cushion of air.

So what's happening?

Magnetism isn't magical – it's just another type of force.
Here's how it works...

Materials are made up of tiny atoms, with even tinier electrons whizzing around them. In some atoms, the electrons create a pulling force. But usually atoms are all jumbled up and point in different directions, so any pulling forces cancel each other out.

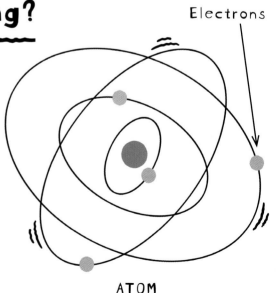

Electrons

ATOM

In a magnetic material, the pulling forces can line up, creating a single bigger pulling force in one direction.

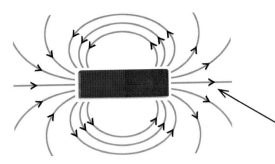

The area of force around the magnet is called the magnetic field.

Push or pull?

Magnets have two ends, called the north and south poles.

North pole

South pole

The north pole of one magnet and the south pole of another magnet will pull, or 'attract' each other.

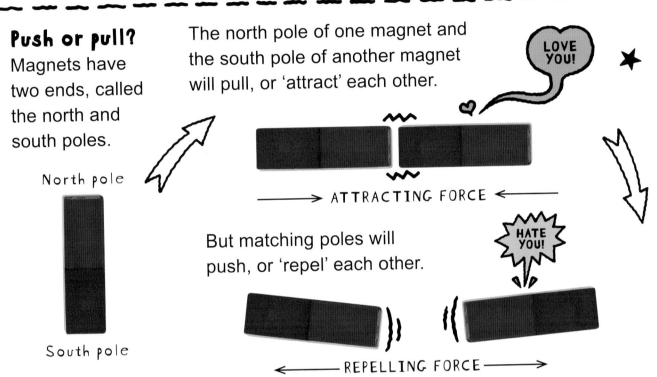

LOVE YOU!

→ ATTRACTING FORCE ←

But matching poles will push, or 'repel' each other.

HATE YOU!

← REPELLING FORCE →

Faraway forces

Magnets can push and pull across a gap, because the pulling forces in the atoms can do this. How this actually works is still not totally understood, even by scientists. But it's not that strange.

If you think about it, magnetism is like gravity (see pages 20-21) – it can pull without touching you.

Magnetic metals

Magnets also attract some metals, like the steel in a paper clip. When a magnet pulls on these metals, they can become magnetic too.

This means you can use one magnet to magnetise a chain of paper clips.

How does the tablecloth trick work?

Can you really pull a tablecloth out from under a set of plates and cups, leaving them all where they were?

The answer is **yes** – but you have to do it right. **DON'T** try this at home! Try the easier experiment opposite instead.

How it's done

To make the trick work, the secret is to pull the tablecloth as hard and suddenly as possible. If you pull it too slowly, everything will get pulled off and...

Smash!

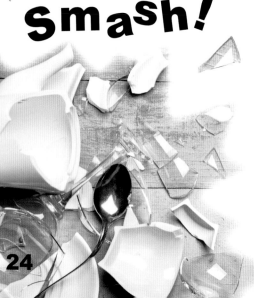

But why?

Inertia

Inertia is one of the laws of motion explained by Isaac Newton (see page 5). It basically means that objects will try to keep doing whatever they're doing. For example, if an object is moving, it will keep going, like this ball...

...unless other forces slow it down, stop it, or change its direction.

Splosh!

Stay still!

If an object is still, it will stay still…

…unless forces act on it to move it...

...LIKE THIS!

Staying on the table

TA-DAAA!

In the tablecloth trick, the objects on the table won't move unless there's a force strong enough to overcome their inertia.

Friction makes the objects grip the tablecloth. If you pull it slowly, this friction makes the objects move with it.

But there isn't enough friction to make the objects move really fast. So if you whip the tablecloth out in a split second, they'll stay still!

(It works best if the tablecloth has a smooth, flat edge.)

Pull the paper

Instead of a tablecloth, try this slightly less risky version...

Cut a piece of paper about the size of a playing card. Put it on top of a clean, dry bottle, and stack several coins on top.

Now try to pull the paper out, leaving the coins on the bottle.

Why can you jump higher on the Moon?

Boing!

Boing!

Boing!

"Walking on the Moon is like walking on a giant trampoline" – according to astronaut Harrison Schmitt, who went there in 1972.

You can jump higher on the Moon, and you fall back down more slowly. But that's not because the Moon is bouncy.

It's because you actually weigh less on the Moon!

What is weight?

You might think your weight is the same wherever you are, but weight doesn't work like that.

Mass: 36 kg
Weight: 36 kg

Your mass stays the same wherever you are. Mass is the amount of matter, or stuff, in an object. So your mass might be 36 kg, for example.

But weight means how much gravity pulls on an object.

On Earth, you'd weigh 36 kg...

but on the Moon you'd weigh much less, because the Moon is smaller and has weaker gravity.

In fact, on the Moon, you'd only weigh about one sixth of what you do on the Earth.

Stuck on Jupiter

If you travelled to a much bigger planet, like Jupiter, where gravity is much stronger, it wouldn't be like a trampoline at all – it would be more like being stuck to the ground.

(Actually, it wouldn't be quite like this, because Jupiter is mostly gas and liquid, so there wouldn't be any solid ground to be stuck to. But if there was, it would be hard to stand up!)

Floating free

As you move further away from a planet (or Moon), the pull of its gravity gets weaker. In outer space, you're so far from any planet that there's hardly any gravity at all – it's called microgravity. So, astronauts in space feel weightless, and can float around in all directions.

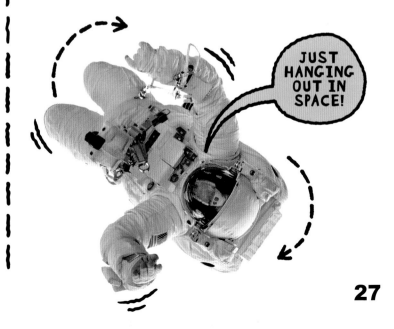

Quick-fire questions

Whooosh!

How do rockets take off?

Rockets work using Newton's famous law of equal and opposite reactions. When a rocket launches, it burns a huge amount of fuel, shooting gases downwards out of its engine at high speed. As the rocket pushes out the gases, the gases push back against the rocket, forcing it upwards.

Is the Earth a giant magnet?

Yes, the Earth has a powerful magnetic field. Liquid iron inside the Earth has electric currents flowing in it, and as the Earth spins, this electricity creates a strong magnetic force.

How do tightrope walkers stay up?

An object can balance if its centre of gravity – the middle point of its mass – is lined up with its base. On a tightrope, your base is very narrow. You have to keep shifting your weight to keep your central point directly above the tightrope.

Why can't we feel air pressure?

The weight of air in the Earth's atmosphere creates a lot of air pressure. We don't notice it because we're used to it, and our bodies have evolved to have a similar pressure inside. However, if you go deep underwater, you feel very squashed, because water pressure is even stronger. But a deep-sea creature like a giant squid or anglerfish feels fine, because it has evolved to cope with that pressure.

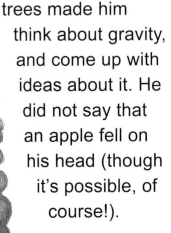

Angler fish

NO PRESSURE!

Did Isaac Newton really discover gravity when an apple fell on his head?

MMM... APPLE PIE!

This is a famous story, but it isn't quite accurate. Everyone knows things fall to the ground, so Newton didn't really 'discover' gravity. However, he did describe how seeing apples falling from trees made him think about gravity, and come up with ideas about it. He did not say that an apple fell on his head (though it's possible, of course!).

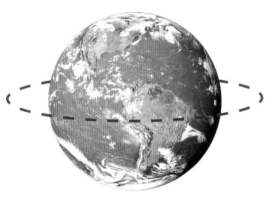

Why can't we feel the Earth spinning?

The Earth rotates once every 24 hours, which means that you're zooming around on it at about 1,000 km/h on average (it varies, depending on how close to the equator you are). However, the Earth's atmosphere is spinning with it, so you don't feel as if you're going fast.

Glossary

Acceleration The way an object speeds up as it moves or falls.

Aerofoil The shape of an aircraft wing that helps to provide lift.

Air pressure The force of the air all around us pressing on people and objects.

Air resistance A force that slows down a moving object as air pushes against it.

Atmosphere The layer of air all around the Earth.

Atom A tiny unit that matter is made up of.

Density How heavy something is for its size.

Drag Another name for air resistance.

Engineer Someone who designs or maintains buildings or other structures.

Evolve To develop and change over time.

Friction A force that slows down or stops objects as they scrape or rub together.

Gravity A force that pulls all objects towards each other.

Inertia The way an object will tend to stay doing what it's doing, whether it's still or moving.

Lift A force that pushes an object, such as an aircraft wing, upwards.

Magnetism A force that makes some objects pull together or push apart.

Mass The amount of matter that an object contains.

Matter The stuff that everything is made up of.

Microgravity Very weak gravity, in which you feel weightless.

Molecules Units of matter made from atoms joined together.

Orbit To circle around another object, for example when a Moon orbits around a planet.

Satellite An object that orbits around another object, especially an artificial satellite such as a space station.

Streamlined A long, pointed shape that helps an object move through air or water more easily.

Surface tension A force that makes molecules at the surface of water pull together, making the water behave as if it has a thin skin.

Upthrust A force that pushes upwards on an object in a liquid or gas.

Further reading

Websites

www.dkfindout.com/uk/science/ forces-and-motion/what-is-force/

Lots of clear, simple forces facts, plus pictures and a quiz.

www.fizzicseducation.com.au/category/150-science- experiments/force-movement-experiments/

Fun forces and movement experiments to try.

www.jamesdysonfoundation.co.uk/content/dam/pdf/JDF_with%20 cover%20challenge-cards_DIGITAL.pdf

Amazing engineering challenges on printable sheets.

www.stevespanglerscience.com/lab/categories/experiments/ forces-and-motion/

Forces and motion activities from Steve Spangler Science.

Books

Extreme Science: Powerful Forces
by Jon Richards and Rob Colson (Wayland, 2020)

Forces of Nature: Experiments with Forces & Magnetism
by Nick Arnold (QEB, 2019)

STEM Activity: Extreme Engineering by Paul Virr (Carlton Kids, 2018)

The Eureka Moment: Isaac Newton and Gravity
by Alex Woolf (Book House, 2019)

How to Be an Engineer by Carol Vorderman (DK, 2018)

Index